MUMS, THE TONGUE, AND PARADISE

poems by

Helen Marie Casey

Finishing Line Press
Georgetown, Kentucky

MUMS, THE TONGUE, AND PARADISE

Copyright © 2022 by Helen Marie Casey
ISBN 979-8-88838-052-9 First Edition
All rights reserved under International and Pan-American Copyright Conventions. No part of this book may be reproduced in any manner whatsoever without written permission from the publisher, except in the case of brief quotations embodied in critical articles and reviews.

ACKNOWLEDGMENTS

Caduceus: The Poets at Art Place—About Heaven, My Father Was Always Unsure
The Comstock Review—Language of Grief
The Larcom Review—Portrait of My Garden in Autumn
The Litchfield Review—Novena
Louisiana Literature—Except that You Lived Long
Minimus: Stories and Poems—Fine Arts
Sojourner: The Women's Forum—Mums, the Tongue, and Paradise
The South Carolina Review—Travel Plans
Tiferet: A Journal of Spiritual Literature—Loaves and Pears

Publisher: Leah Huete de Maines
Editor: Christen Kincaid
Cover Art: Anita Kurth
Author Photo: Dean Casey
Cover Design: Elizabeth Maines McCleavy

Order online: www.finishinglinepress.com
also available on amazon.com

Author inquiries and mail orders:
Finishing Line Press
PO Box 1626
Georgetown, Kentucky 40324
USA

Table of Contents

Adagio 1

Listening 2

It Is Dark Within 3

Between Us 4

The Murdered Boy 5

Fine Arts 6

Ite, Missa Est 7

Picasso's Minotaur 8

The White Butterfly 9

About Heaven, My Father Was Always Unsure 10

After Dark 11

Wimpled Nuns 12

Loaves and Pears 13

The Devil's Right Hand 14

Novena 15

August 16

Cherub 17

Come Home 18

Mums, the Tongue, and Paradise 19

Sculpting God 20

Except that You Lived Long 21

Travel Plans 22

Portrait of My Garden in Autumn 23

On the Anniversary of Your Death 24

Always for Dean

Adagio

Everywhere the yellow of death grips leaves.
When the last has fallen, we see the beauty of lack.
We see how adornment deceives us, how superfluous
splendor's flame, the wild appeal of skeletal relief.

Bare essentials, the world leaving us, it is only you
I want, weight of all that claims us released, you and I
dizzy in our turning, all that remains pared away,
the two of us in the shadow of trees letting go.

Listening

The loneliness of trees in winter is imagined.
What they miss is not the sun. Nor leaves.
Nor color's shout. They learn to hug the snow,
to bend as they must, to shed a limb.
There will be birds now and then, as there are today,
some in transit to another place. In the gutters
and rainspouts, some seeds will draw the jays.
They, too, will leave when ice coats the sills and eaves.
What the trees tell each other we can only guess.
Exposed branches lean toward the stuttering winds,
unafraid. Their laments are whispered.
We cannot hear what they have to tell us.

It Is Dark Within

Even the stillness is pregnant, sky uncertain,
all the gods somewhere else, perhaps in consultation,
trees putting on spring and whistling, or so I imagine.
Winter is long. Trees survive to dress again.
Like us—weathered, a bit notched—they grow
selective, see what they want to see, or so I imagine.
They are not like the iris, diaphanous, here today
and gone tomorrow, wildly insouciant. Leggy.
The trees I love close ranks, or so I imagine.
It is dark within the stand of oaks, maples, pines,
but not silent. Squirrels make springboards of branches.
Night comes. Frogs, cicadas, bats, and owls debate, or so I imagine.
These trees will be here when we are gone, taller, a few limbs
missing. The whispering will go on, younger cardinals arriving
to conceal themselves in leafy shade, happy, or so I imagine.

Between Us

The shade trees huddle, secrets they own theirs
alone. Sky white as the fright of finches
says nothing, waiting, time of no more consequence
than the vaporous contrail, less tangible than the yellow begonia
that hugs the shade, slipping over the basket's side. Earth draws
every one of us down, soil rich, dark, welcoming. The trees
will not stop the sibilant flutter of what they tell. We will not
cease listening for what we will never know.

The Murdered Boy

I looked forward to it, the rain hitting the porch
like hail, the presence of something not myself
doing what it was given to do. I could go a long time
thinking the earth at peace with itself, content to let go
restraint. Then comes the thunder. One boy stabs another
to death. Mere kids. I'd like to say the earth groans.
It doesn't. Winter earth grows a hard shell.
We stand numbly staring where no sound penetrates
and flowers do not grow.

Fine Arts

The naked ladies at the pool powder their breasts, their bellies, between their legs, rub their skin with unguents, decorate their faces, dress. They do not look beyond the trees.
They do not see the satyrs waiting, as if they have all the time in the world.

When buying pears, choose firm, smooth, unblemished fruit like *Winter Nelis*, round and plump with medium-brown skin. Or *Bartlett*, bell-shaped, sometimes blushed with pale red.

Look. The mother squirrel uses her paws to put her hairless baby in her mouth. She transports him down the tree, runs behind the house, and into the woods. For safety. Elsewhere, foggy nights, salamanders clog the streets, homing toward vernal pools. Reckless nights like these, friends come apart. Rootbound. Dead limbs. Trees hunch in waltz time, desire fragile. Sometimes, we do not know enough. We do not. Saffron, red stigma of the flowering crocus. Stigma. A spot on the skin that bleeds.

Ite, Missa Est

They do not speak the language of grief, these wind-wrapped
trees. They do not keen the losses, desiccation inevitable,
endings more necessary than beginnings. They live
otherwise, each moment its own journey, the future
a figment of alternate imaginations. I am not like trees
dropping their glory for winter. Uncomplaining. I miss
every leaf, every pine needle, every limb that rots and drops.
The scarlet ones hold on and on, stubborn. The Japanese Maple
gives up everything at once. I shall insist on fighting,
the last gasp of color furious. Illuminating.

Picasso's Minotaur

In the City of Light, even the statues kiss.
They never lose their rapture, these figures, fractured
marble, bliss lifting their nipples, their lips, their legs.

Peacocks preen in the mid-day heat of the Bois de Boulogne.
The peahens ignore them. Those pretty males scream across the gardens.
Elsewhere, inside the *musée*, Picasso is on the wall and the lines are long.

The Minotaur, lascivious, lowers himself. Only his sad eyes
tell us he knows exactly what he does. He would like to be sorry.
He would like to forget her indelible, purple scream.

The White Butterfly

Not much laughter this wormy day, chipmunks oblivious
to everything but their own running, their burrows, and we absent,
except to grief, not wishing for anything but mindless joy,
hands cupped for sorrows that will surely come hobbling
toward us. The white butterfly whose name I do not know
passes, of no more moment than Icarus's silent fall. How much
of what we have lost returns? How much is less than ash
under foot? Who can say what else the empty spaces might have held?

About Heaven, My Father Was Always Unsure

He knew bears. Did contest with them. The one
that trashed his cabin outlived my father. The last deer
he shot came looking for the bullet. He stood still,
that deer, right outside the screen door, waiting
for my Dad to bag one more story. Fish were more
private. When he reeled them in, it was almost two
companions on the same team. About birds he was
certain. He could wait as long as it took for the pheasant,
the quail, or the emerald-necked teal. Once only
I set out with him in the cold morning, marsh grass tall.
When blood began to drain down my legs, he made me
wait in the blind alone. Did he remember every missed
opportunity, his understanding of what we cannot count on
as strong as his kinship with the bear, the stubborn one
that returns, prepared to mark my father's place?

After Dark

Night comes and we let down everything,
the ladder of sleep slippery. Both hands steer us
into the dark, dreams the only stars available,
your body a bridge to everywhere. Tree frogs
disturb the night with song. Half-asleep,
you call my name. I touch the pain
knotted at the tip of your spine. I curl
into a quarter moon to cradle you, rungs
of our descent uneven as shark's teeth,
shades flapping as we enter space and land
that are nothing but absence. Asleep, we are
who we are and who we might be if time,
the dragon who toys with us, were friendlier.
Released between worlds, we spread the wings
we do not have, fly into love and out of it, see
what isn't there as we have never seen before.

Wimpled Nuns

The first was born at home. I came surrounded
by nuns, the hospital sterile, my mother not yet twenty,
more babies waiting their turn until my mother did not
want any more babies. I walked in the shadow
of all those wimpled nuns. I wanted
God and words, settled for questions. Even now
I puzzle meaning and chew facts. I am looking
for sound and sense. When I am blindsided
by beauty, I am speechless. Between raindrops
I stand wanting what will never be.

Loaves and Pears

I never write father poems
and I don't often write about God.
I have a father
and I believe there is a God.
I write love poems
certain that words can never envelope love.
I chew memory
and set the bitter seeds aside.
I shape pain
turning it like the pear on the windowsill
in love with the sun.
I shape it, like dough, into a loaf.
I let the poem rise
the one that wants to be about my father.

The Devil's Right Hand

> *Pierre de Giac était beau, brave jusqu'à la folie, fourbe, séduisant et terrible.*
> —Philippe Erlanger

The man who sold his hand to the devil was afraid
of no man. The right hand, the one he bargained with,
he used to disembowel his enemies and cut down his wife, big
with child. He strung her beneath his horse and rode her
to death. The man who sold his hand to the devil was afraid
of no man. He bedded another man's wife. Naked, he was taken
to the river's edge in the Year of Our Lord 1427. Before they tied him
in a sack to drown him, he looked for Satan. With a cold eye,
he begged a single mercy of the Christian men who held him.
Pierre de Giac, the man who sold his hand to the devil was afraid
of no man. The warrior held up the ruthless right hand he owed.
Chop it off. The water rose around him before it resumed
its course, new cargo less interesting than the infernal weather
that traipsed, with no discernible malice, along the turbulent shores.

Novena

Random murder is hardly a fit subject but this is your poem
and there you are, decaying. Sugar cane conceals your body.
I cry for both of us, fear taking me where I do not want to go,
always back, the moment of surprise, the moment you knew
it was over, his eyes dead cold, no air getting past his fingers,
your neck squeezed until you no longer knew anything.
And all the while we prayed and searched.
Six days. You were *vanished*, which holds hope
the way *dead* doesn't.

After they found you, the papers said it was your fault.
You should have known better. Jogging alone on a sunny morning,
they said, was stupid. I see it your way. Breaking a sweat,
keeping your body in shape, watching the sun fill the sky:
who could want anything more?

I keep picturing myself there, sharing, as college roommates will.
I remember you, sophomore year, leaning over, testing,
to be sure no one could see anything you didn't want them to see.
We did everything we were supposed to—waited, married, had children.
Our problem, Joan, is that we believed.
We believed in *the promises,*
Nine First Fridays, nine acts of fidelity, the guarantee
we would die in our own beds. Safe.
But what did we know?

August

Behind my back animals eat
the garden, break the necks
of lilies, chew in the dark.

I plant asters, yarrow, lilacs,
more lilies. I watch the garden
hesitate.

Impatiens grows beside the bleeding
hearts, black-eyed Susans nudge
snapdragons. Roses but no lilies.

Some fragrance. Some color. Some death.
That is the way of birthdays.

Cherub

There is no trap door and I am not Alice tall and small.
I do not meet a cat whose smile outlasts his wisdom
nor do I know where the fat winged cherub lives, except
somewhere between Chopin and Lizst. Autumn plays tag
and I am it, desiccation riding on the back of the hag
who turns the pages. *Pèlerinages*, the musician called his
journeying, engraving melancholy in every holy space,
stillness etched within his notes. There is no loneliness
quite like death. In the morning there is no morning.
Evenings leave their pink. In between, the living, seldom
startled, wander aimlessly. I miss you, even when
you are here. Touching, we almost speak what we need,
the heart migratory, our journeys serendipitous. Words do not
work hard enough, flapping through the manzanitas, hungry,
unrequited. What can we tell them about the famished soul, about
the meaning of dinner at the hotel, *crème brûlée, espresso*, a bit of dark
chocolate, you incandescing, your mouth happy? What can we tell?

Come Home

For William Stafford's Artist

The house is alive with sound. Remember the branches
scraping the bedroom windows, wanting to come inside?

Now and again a squirrel makes it and I do what I always do,
react like a crazy woman facing a cougar in her own backyard.

I turn porch lights on when I'm alone,
light: a stand against cowardice of all kinds.

The birdfeeder hangs by a frayed rope
and the remains of peonies look like they'll never recover.

Remember the place where you raised pigeons,
the slope forested with leaves?

Two hawks own the sky overhead
and the Japanese maples have fallen asleep.

Mums, the Tongue, and Paradise

Only the mums want to go on
shouting. For the rest, dullness and death.
If they harbor memory, we do not know it
or want to know it. We are not like the maple,
splendid before it shrivels. We are not
like the sedum that learns to blend or the crows
ceaselessly complaining. We are vessels of solitude,
mooring uncertain. Lonely as that first Adam
searching for names, evolving the sounds *rhino, warthog,
dove*, he fell into love with what the tongue
could fashion. It would be some time before he learned
the limits, what words cannot undo.

Sculpting God

Inside the Isabella Stewart Gardner Museum

There, in the hallway of the palazzo, his helmet jaunty
as a fedora, the knight empties his bucket and water douses
the keep, which is not on fire. Blame it on art, the way
we cannot help what we see, the followers of Jesus in sumptuous
silks, the Virgin lifting her apple breast to the hungry lips,
her baby plump, naked, and—the angel announced—her God though,
when He hammers nails with John, He is one cousin
sporting with another. We cannot help what we see, the Infant
everywhere. Sometimes He is bread, sometimes returned to his mother,
dead as marble and more mysterious. She was reading,
the artist tells us, when Gabriel arrived with news. She did not
look up. The long halls of the palace shifted, the six-foot-high wings,
crenellated, were not unlike the sheen of abalone, his hair fastened
at the neck, braided. What does she think now, the Madonna,
her heart fissured, her marbled arms cold as Montana?

Except that You Lived Long

Your name lies beside his and the view
from your part of the hill is what you'd like
if you chose to look. Where are you
when we call your name? Where are you
when your husband says, "I can't find Mom
anywhere" and reaches for you, time an anchor?
The scarlet tanager commands attention
while you need nothing we know
how to offer, not incense, not jewels,
not even the tea-roses you once loved. We turn
to prayer, *Requiem aeternam dona eis, Domine.*
We turn to each other. We climb up the hill,
the stone with your name and your dates
telling little that matters.

Travel Plans

The years are on a journey and I follow, often late for the craft
I need, running for my life. Today I am a parachute,
wind enough to carry me to the Neva, the windows of the palace
curtained, love a possibility there by the Griboedeva
where the paintbox Church of the Resurrection sees everything
and nothing changes. White nights, swallows sail the courtyards.
And crows. I am at the window listening and no one knows
what lies beyond. The icons wear circles under their eyes,
their sad faces a reminder of how hard it is
to know. Incense rises to the God who sees our coming in
and our going out. I cross myself and wait
in the darkness that moves at its own awful pace.

Portrait of My Garden in Autumn

My wild blue hydrangea lets go, its veins
tired of so much plumage. Cardinals sing.
Whitewashed sky is silent. Some wind.
Then the stillness. My good friend will not
live the year.   He harvests his energy,
what little there is of it, as if it can
make a difference, as if he can live to fathom
the forces unraveling a perfectly good system,
can find a mathematical equivalent. He is now
on the other side of language and thin
as the laconic poppy that will not grow. I want
to know if there is clarity before the end or if,
like the asters, he comes to know nothing
but the cold, the fierce, silent cold.

On the Anniversary of Your Death

In the end, Emily, we are *all* alone,
living more in our mind
than anyone surmises.
We ravel thought,
transforming one idea
into its opposite, writing
our way for no one
so much as ourselves.
We must create to live.
The world longs
to be deciphered, or
is it the other way
around—we long
to decipher the world?
Finding the word
that works
becomes our passion,
appetites for solitude,
and books, insatiable.
We must craft
our own landscape the way
we piece a quilt, one tentative
seam after another,
endless variations
on death and possibility.
As for love, we find ourselves
listing, as if in the act of revision,
starting to say— then doubting—
what art can penetrate,
what mortals can divine.

Helen Marie Casey is a New England writer whose chapbooks include: *Fragrance Upon His Lips*, *Inconsiderate Madness*, *Zero Degrees* and *You Kept Your Secrets*. She has also written *My Dear Girl: The Art of Florence Hosmer*, and *Portland's Compromise: The Colored School 1867-1872*. She won the 2005 Black River Chapbook competition and the 14th National Poet Hunt of *The MacGuffin*. She was a semifinalist in the 2021 Tomaz Salamun Prize competition. Her work has appeared in several journals, including, among others: *Louisiana Literature, The Paterson Literary Review, The MacGuffin, The South Carolina Review, Calyx, CT Review, Larcom Review, Laurel Review, Comstock Review, Tiferet, Christian Century,* and the *Worcester Review*.

www.ingramcontent.com/pod-product-compliance
Lightning Source LLC
Chambersburg PA
CBHW022128090426
42743CB00008B/1051